HELLO, FISH!

VISITING THE CORAL REEF

by Sylvia A. Earle

with photographs by Wolcott Henry

NATIONAL GEOGRAPHIC SOCIETY

Washington, D.C.

For the fish,
for all who wish fish well,
for Wolcott, and for two fish-watchers to be:
Deirdra Henry McKelvy and Taylor Earle Griffith
— Sylvia Earle

To Sylvia and Angel,
for your inspiration and support,
and to the next generation of those dedicated to exploring
and protecting the marine world
— Wolcott Henry

Text copyright © 1999 Sylvia A. Earle
Photographs (except as otherwise credited) copyright © 1999 Wolcott Henry
First paperback edition 2001

Published by the National Geographic Society.

Book design by Patrick Collins
Special thanks to Paul Humann for fish identification; to Carl Mehler, Director of Maps, Book Division;
and to Michelle H. Picard, Map Production

Library of Congress Cataloging-in-Publication Data
Earle, Sylvia A., 1935—
Hello, Fish! / by Sylvia A. Earle : with photographs by Wolcott Henry.
p. cm.
Summary: An underwater explorer takes a tour of the ocean and introduces such fish
as the damselfish, stargazer, and brown goby.
ISBN 0-7922-7103-3 (hardcover) ISBN: 0-7922-6697-8 (paperback)
1. Fishes—Juvenile literature. [1. Fishes.] I. Henry, Wolcott, ill. II. Title.
QL617.2.E36 1999
597—dc21   98-38380

Printed in the United States of America

Front cover: Clownfish in an anemone
Back cover: Yellowtail snapper watching Sylvia Earle read a book about fish.
Title page: Yellow blenny

The world's largest nonprofit scientific and educational organization, the National Geographic Society was founded in 1888 "for the increase and diffusion of geographic knowledge." Since then it has supported scientific exploration and spread information to its more than eight million members worldwide. The National Geographic Society educates and inspires millions every day through magazines, books, television programs, videos, maps and atlases, research grants, the National Geographic Bee, teacher workshops, and innovative classroom materials. The Society is supported through membership dues, charitable donations, and income from the sale of its educational products. Members receive NATIONAL GEOGRAPHIC magazine—the Society's official journal—discounts on Society products and other benefits. For more information about the National Geographic Society, its educational programs and publications, and ways to support its work, please call 1-800-NGS-LINE (647-5463) or write to the following address:

NATIONAL GEOGRAPHIC SOCIETY
1145 17th Street N.W.
Washington, D.C. 20036-4688
U.S.A.

Visit the Society's Web site: www.nationalgeographic.com

PRINTED IN THE UNITED STATES OF AMERICA

8903

NORTH
AMERICA

EUROPE

ASIA

PACIFIC
OCEAN

PACIFIC

OCEAN

ATLANTIC

OCEAN

AFRICA

EQUATOR

SOUTH
AMERICA

INDIAN

OCEAN

AUSTRALIA

CORAL REEF

ANTARCTICA

Of all the kinds of creatures that have backbones—people,
frogs, snakes, and birds to name a few—fish are the most
numerous. They have gills to help them breathe, scales to
protect their skin, and fins for swimming through the waters of
the world. All of the fish in this book live in and around coral
reefs. These rocklike structures, which take thousands of years to
form, are made up of billions of skeletons from tiny animals
called corals. These reefs, shown in orange on the map, flourish
in shallow areas of warm ocean waters. You will discover,
as you read this book, that reef fish come in a variety of shapes,
colors, and sizes. Each has its own special place in the
wondrous world of the coral reef.

If you wonder what fish do all day
and how they spend their nights,
come glide with me into the sea.
We'll say hello to creatures who
make their home in a realm of blue.

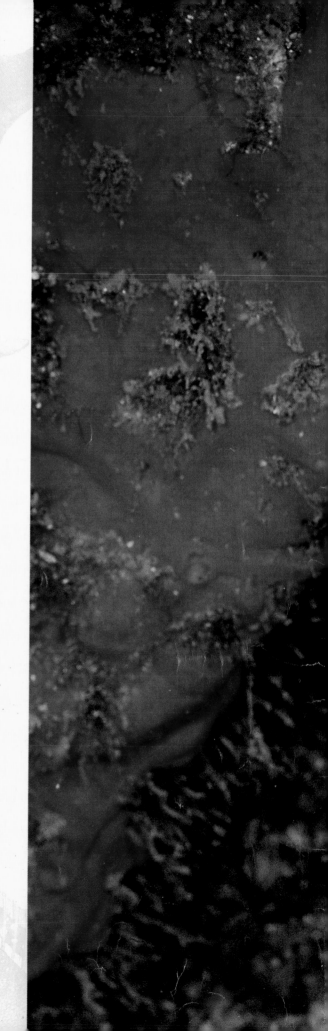

SPOTTED MORAY
I often stop and play with morays.
I've even hugged a few!

Moray eels can be dangerous, though,

if you happen to be a small fish or octopus.

Watch out!

You could become an eel meal!

But people aren't on their menu.

In fact, these gentle and curious fish

remind me of kittens.

It's easy to see why this one

is called a spotted moray,

a fine name for a totally freckled fish.

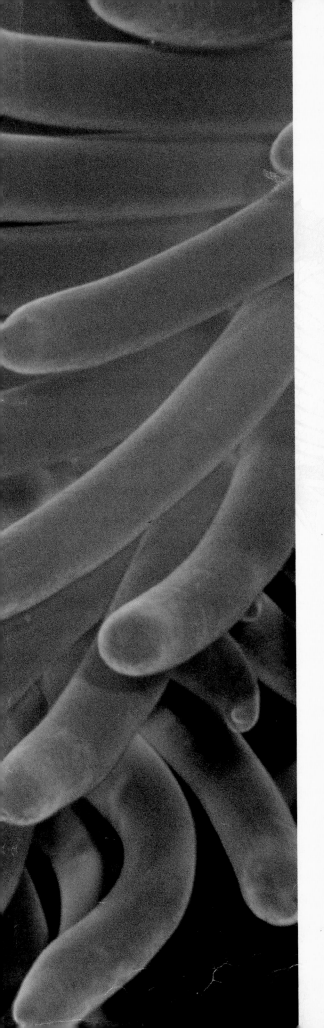

CLOWNFISH

In an anemone's soft, slippery arms
A clownfish hides as large fish pass by.

It looks as though this fish

might be in trouble

among the stinging tentacles

of a sea anemone. But no!

This is a clownfish,

one of dozens of kinds of small fish

that actually make their homes

and raise their families

in places that are deadly to other creatures.

Clownfish coat their fins and scales

with a wonderful kind of slimy goo

that keeps them from being stung.

STARGAZER

Now you see it, now you don't.
Is it a pile of pebbles and sand, or a fish?

With clever camouflage

stargazers fool big fish that might want to eat them.

They also trick the little fish they want to eat.

When something tasty swims by,

that big, toothy mouth quickly opens

and gulps down a meal.

With eyes that always look up,

it's easy to see why these fish are called stargazers.

But, since they live in the sea,

maybe they should be called starfish gazers!

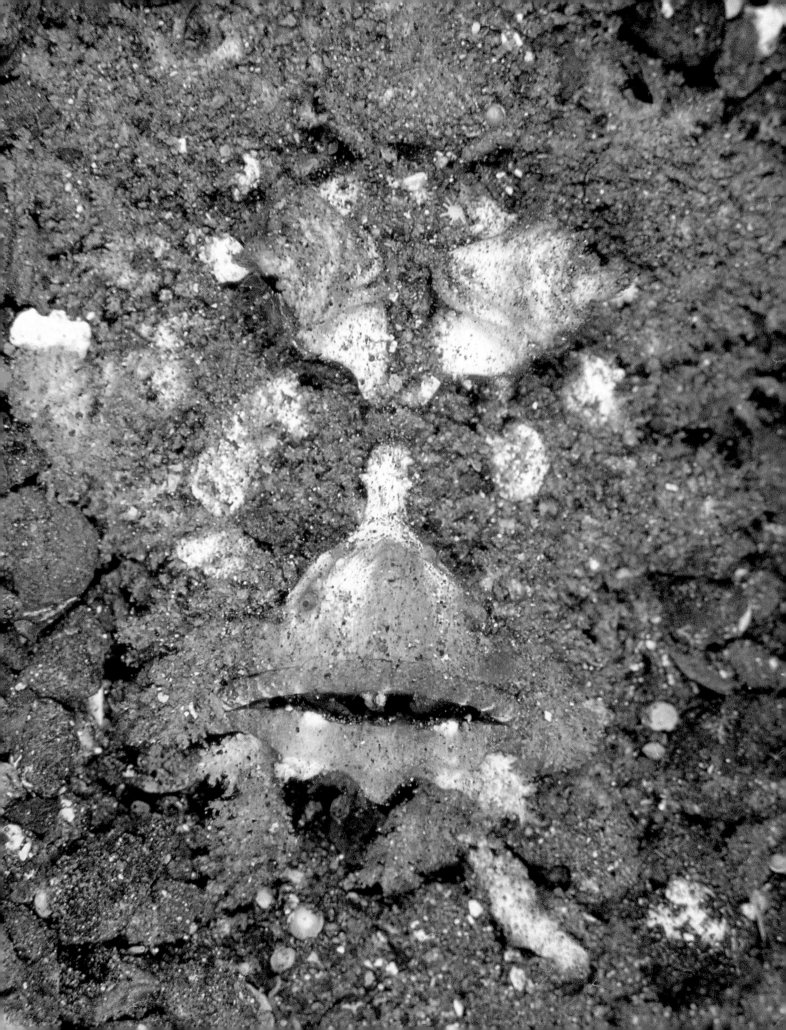

SILVERTIP SHARK
A silver swimmer in the reef, this shark
Is one of the ancient ocean dwellers.

If you could go back in time

300 million years,

you would find no whales,

no dolphins, no seals,

no elephants, no birds,

or trees or flowers or grass.

But there would be sharks in the sea.

Many people are afraid of sharks,

but of the more than 350 kinds now known,

very few ever even nibble on us.

People kill so many sharks, though,

that some kinds may soon be gone forever.

Let's take care so the sea can always be

home to sharks.

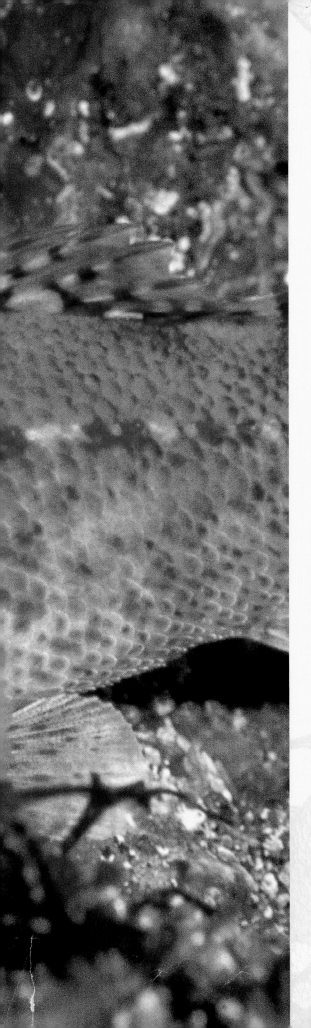

RAINBOW SCORPIONFISH

Hovering still against the reef,
A scorpionfish hides.

You might think that a red fish

would be easy to find in a blue ocean.

But against colorful sponges and corals,

this scorpionfish blends right in.

His spiny fins are a good defense,

but if you don't hurt him,

he won't hurt you.

His large, beautiful eyes

help him find his way around in the sea.

While I watch him, he watches me.

BROWN GOBY

Look closely to find little gobies,
Like this one peeking out at you.

This brown goby

may venture out a short distance

from his adopted home,

an empty worm tube.

But at the first hint of danger,

he'll dive back into shelter for safety.

Like most gobies,

this one props himself up

on the small fins under his chin

when he wants to look out

at the world.

DAMSELFISH

This jewel-like creature with
Blue-and-gold eyes is a damselfish.

It is one in a family

of hundreds of creatures

most commonly found in tropical seas

around coral reefs.

Most are no bigger than your hand,

but inside that sheath of sleek scales

is a very tough fish.

When provoked, damselfish

will chase away creatures

many times their size—

even me!

RED GOBY

This red goby has a sweeping tail
And on its back a ruby sail!

I sometimes find these fish

with a magnifying glass.

Can you imagine that within a body

no bigger than your little finger

there can be teeth and eyes

and a backbone, stomach, heart, and tongue,

and all the other things fish need to live?

Gobies eat tiny shrimplike creatures.

Most spend their time in a small area

and can live for years in a single shell.

STRIPED CATFISH
Cats aren't the only creatures
Famous for their whiskers!

Catfish whiskers are soft and sensitive—

very useful feelers, especially in the dark.

There are hundreds of kinds of catfish

in the ocean and in some lakes,

rivers, and streams.

None have scales—quite unusual for fish!

None have fur, either, of course.

But all have gills like other fish.

Little catfish tend to stay together.

Probably they're safer than they would be

if each one swam around the reef alone.

FROGFISH

With bulbous eyes and slippery skin,
This must be the well-named frogfish!

Actually, all frogs and all of the 20,000 or so kinds of fish

and all of the 9,000 kinds of birds

and all of the thousands of kinds of mammals

and all turtles and lizards and snakes have something in common.

We all have backbones—vertebrae—

unlike most of the rest of life on Earth.

Beetles don't, crabs don't, starfish don't, octopuses don't,

nor do jellyfish, of course!

But frogs and fish and people everywhere do—

including you!

Spotted Stingray

Graceful, gentle creatures, rays glide
Through the sea like giant butterflies.

Spotted stingrays pause now and then

to dine on clams, snails, and other

small animals that live in soft sand or mud

on the seafloor.

Many kinds of rays and

their toothy relatives—the sharks—

live in the oceans of the world.

Millions of years ago

rays and sharks were swimming

in the deep sea.

And, they still are!

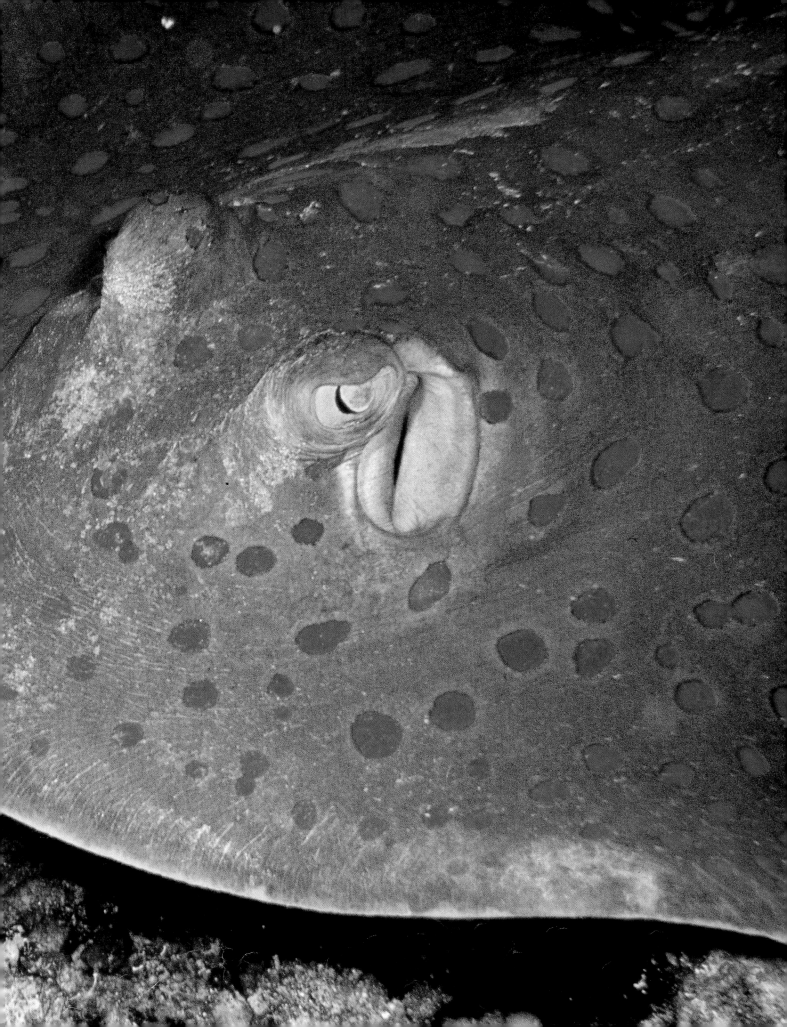

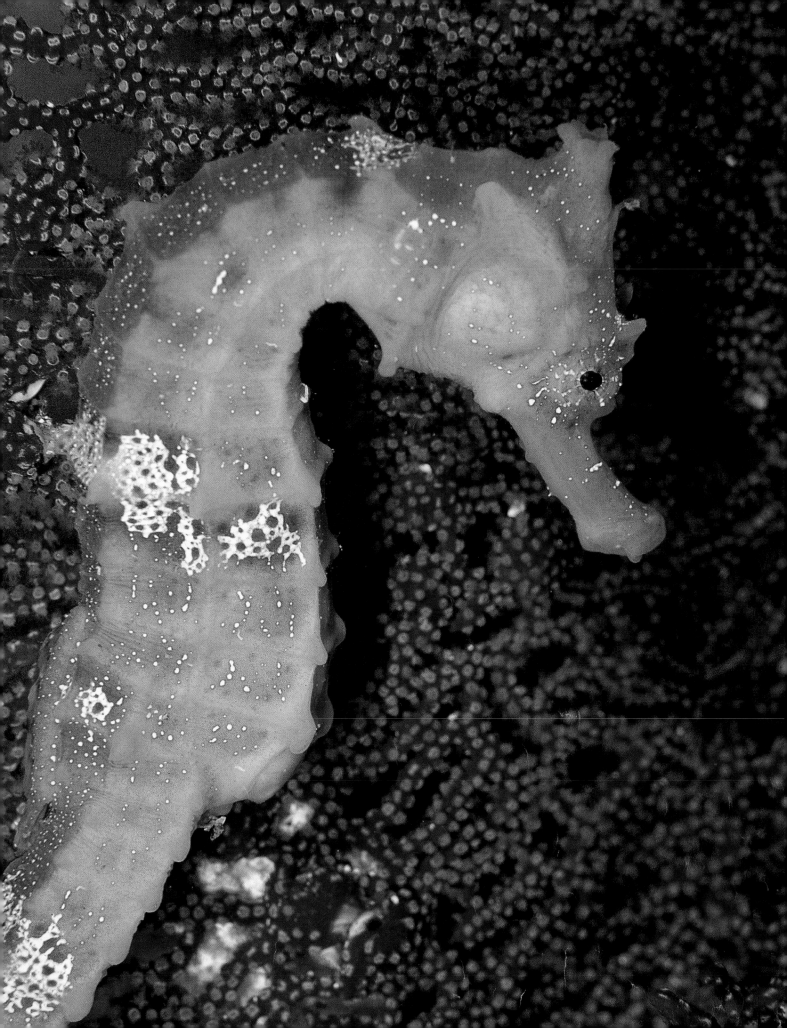

SEAHORSE

This curvy fish—what could it be?
A seahorse, with room to roam the sea.

Seahorses are small fish with large eyes.

They have a big appetite for tiny crustaceans.

Like people, they choose partners for life.

They usually stay together, even during stormy weather.

Seahorse mothers lay their eggs in special pouches

that seahorse fathers have in their bellies.

Weeks later, fully formed little fish

swim out of the pouches into the sea—

ready to grow up

and find partners of their own.

Great Barracuda

Red Lizardfish

Scrawled Cowfish

Queen Angelfish

School of Silversides

NOW THAT YOU'VE MET
A FEW OF MY FRIENDS,
I HOPE YOU'LL LEARN MORE
ABOUT THE SEA WHERE THEY LIVE.

Leopard Blenny

Queen Parrotfish

Spanish Hogfish

SYLVIA A. EARLE

Sylvia Earle is a marine biologist, author, lecturer, and ocean explorer. She is the National Geographic Society's Explorer-in-Residence for 1998 and 1999. As part of the Sustainable Seas Expeditions launched in 1998 with Society support, Earle plans to dive in all 12 U.S. marine sanctuaries. Called "Her Deepness" by the *New York Times*, Sylvia Earle has a B.S. from Florida State University and a Ph.D. from Duke University, as well as numerous honorary doctorates. When not underwater, Sylvia Earle lives in Oakland, California.

NATALIE FOBES

WOLCOTT HENRY

Wolcott Henry is an underwater photographer who has explored coral reef areas all over the world, including Indonesia, Papua New Guinea, the Galápagos Islands, Hawaii, and the Florida Keys. He is president of the Curtis and Edith Munson Foundation, an organization that supports marine conservation in North America. Henry's photographs are often used by nonprofit groups to communicate the importance of coral reefs. He lives in Washington, D.C.